THROUGH
the
HORIZON

THROUGH the HORIZON

Oluwasanmi Fademi

Copyright ©2018 Oluwasanmi Fademi

ISBN: 978-978-963-999-1

All rights reserved.
No part of this book may be reproduced, distributed, stored in a retrieval system or transmitted, in any form or by any means, electronic, electrostatic, magnetic tape, mechanical, photocopying, recording or otherwise without prior written permission from the Publisher.
For information about permission to reproduce selections from this book, write to *info@wrr.ng*
National Library of Nigeria Cataloguing-in-Publication Data

Printed and Published in Nigeria by:
Words Rhymes & Rhythm Limited
Suite C309, Global Plaza Plot 366, Obafemi Awolowo Way, Jabi District, Abuja, Nigeria.
08169027757, 08060109295
www.wrr.ng

TABLE OF CONTENTS

TABLE OF CONTENTS 5
DEDICATION 7
ACKNOWLEDGEMENTS 8
AWAKENING 9
BEAUTIFUL MORNING 10
BALANCE...13
A MOTHER'S THROES 14
COMPANIONSHIP 15
HOPE AND DESPAIR...16
FAITH 17
DIRGE...19
JIGSAW PUZZLE 20
HAPPINESS...21
CRUSHED 22
CHOICES...23
DAYS 24
ADULATION 25
POKER FACE...27
LOVE 28
LIFE 29
THE PAIN BARRIER..30
WONDER WOMAN 31
THE FORLORN STRANGER....................................32
THE ILLUSION 34
THE ULTIMATE GIFT...36
THE DOLOROUS HYMN...38
THE PAST 40
VIRTUE...41
MY THUMBELINA 42
SMITTEN 43
THE TRAGEDY OF MY HEART 44
AFRICA 46

MIST	48
DECADES	50
INNER DEMONS	51
NUMB	52
DOXOLOGY	53
MY MUSE	54
ODE TO A FRIEND	55
THE ROMANTIC	56
BATTLEFIELD ODE	57
THE PILGRIM'S BAGGAGE	59
THE DEMISE	60

DEDICATION

for My Dad
    my number one fan....

"Horizons will not come to you; you must go to the horizons!"

— **Mehmet Murat ildan**

AWAKENING

A façade of reality,
An illusion to the genuine,
That is what life often fills the head with,
But like a needle to an inflated balloon,
An exasperated gush of air yearning for freedom,
It pops and the fantasies in my head fizzles out,
Jerking me angrily back to reality,
The anguish and raucous clutter of life,
Ushers me into a new dawn once again,
And I gently murmur to myself,
"Oh... it's a morning,
Thank God I'm awake".

BEAUTIFUL MORNING

It was a beautiful morning,
A clear blue sky,
With the wind whistling gently,
I could hear it calling as it rustles the trees,
And even the birds chirped melodiously,
A wonderful morning it truly is.

Just lying in my bed,
With no real desire to get up to do anything,
I can't even think of what to do,
I dare not think about it,
My thoughts might ruin the beauty of the morning.

In my soliloquy the door jerks open,
And the maids troop in,
They come at me and gently lift me from my bed,
And help me to the bath tub,
They clean me up and drape me in my best Sunday suit,
My disposition shows I long for my bed,
And gently once more,
I was returned to my bed.

What hunk of butlers and waiters serve me so,
I still refused to be bothered about getting up,

And in comes my stroller,
Gently they lift me and put me in my stroller,
And wheel me out to the living room.

Today must be my birthday,
That will describe the surprise party,
And the guests cluttering in my living room,
I could feel their gaze piercing my soul,
As they all come to me and whisper their greetings,
Some couldn't hold back their tears,
I smiled to myself and took all these in,
Tears of joys trickling down their faces,
That I told myself and got comfortable in my stroller.

My chauffeur comes at me,
And wheels me to the car,
So much roses and flowers donning my every step,
A script from the movies for royals,
This birthday will stay with me forever,
I silently thought to myself.

A church service to commemorate my day is next,
Even the minister can't help whispering close to my ears,
And you should hear the glorious things he said about me,
I glowed internally,

As I saw envy creep into some faces,
    what a beautiful day.

The stress of the day finally begin to get to me,
I must rest again I thought to myself,
As my eyes struggle to stay open,
Sleep begins to creep in,
A virtuoso day must come to an end.
I fail to notice my stroller close in on me,
As I lay perfectly still in it,
My eyes closed in deep slumber,
And my stroller gently lowered down,
The day has been memorable and beautiful,
I say to myself,
I do not notice my stroller being dropped,
Six feet below as it steadies on the earth,
I hear nothing more,
As I dozed off,
Resting till the end of days.

BALANCE

The illusion of time,
Mocks the harsh reality of eternity,
Life remains shrouded in mystery,
Death no more than a chilling fable,
A trinity of boundless infinity.

I lie awake in bed,
In deep soliloquy,
Pondering the affairs of men,
The vanity gnawing at their hearts,
And the futility of their wisdom.

What makes one greater than the other?
Who decides the noble and the plebes?
By whose order do one stands as moral?
And another deemed immoral,
A world so strife with inequality.

My heart fumes at the injustice,
My eyes cringe at the horrors,
As I watch the failures of men,
Gets christened with a million names,
And we all merry in its bland inanity.

A MOTHER'S THROES

A still calmness,
A peace that transcends,
A soothing relief to the scorching pain,
A coolness that envelopes,
As it births life.

The still silence shatters,
As tears well up,
And all that seem to niggle,
Vanishes like it never was,
As the piercing cry filters through.

Exasperated sighs echoes across,
Laden with a visible air of happiness,
And love so thick that it smothers,
That only one-----who wrung in pain,
Can aptly describe.......
The throes of motherhood.

COMPANIONSHIP

How my heart aches,
What price do I have to pay?
To secure true companionship,
One that shall heal my aching heart,
And spread its warmth across my ailing body.

Could it be debasement I feel?
Or the bitterness that seems to be rooted within,
Compromise is what I have thought this to be,
For the love I bear outweighs all these,
And should suffer all these to strengthen it.

At what point does it end?
At what point does it all go away,
The exploitation of my heart for the search for companionship,
When do I wear my esteem back on with pride?
My heart can take no more of this extortion.

Unconditional love was I birthed with,
Eternal respect was I adorned with,
But I spat on this with bile,
Only to be scorned by the ones I yearned for,
To my cradle I shall return,
A baby once more in the arms of my family.

HOPE AND DESPAIR

A longing for peace,
A cry for help,
A scourging lease,
Turns one to an unendurable whelp,
Leading an excuse of a life.

A palpable respite,
Bears a promise of a new dawn,
And the drowning of the bitter spite,
Ushers in a bright new morn,
Culminating in a wishful end to a scathing apocalypse.

The whooping effervescence,
Unleashes an excruciating nightmare of desired light,
As I awake with a prayerful fervent,
Banishing and casting aside my demons and fright,
Longing for death; a leeway to an inglorious existence.

FAITH

What is faith? I wonder,
The belief in the unseen,
The bible helps us in giving a beautiful and coherent definition,
"It is the assurance of things hoped for,
And convictions of things not seen"
On this foundation,
We build our trust in God,
And continuously rebuke the evil works of the devil.

If faith is the belief in the unseen,
Then there remains a lot to be said,
There remains a lot to be believed in,
The belief that our death walks side by side with our life,
The belief that just beside our maligned failure,
Lies our esteemed success,
The belief that our sadness is just a mirror of our happiness.

Our faith re-assures us,
That we are whatever we choose to believe we are,
That there is enough warmth and love for everyone,
That we are all the same despite skin color and religion,

That we will always be appreciated and loved,
That we are all mortals,
And from dust we came,
And to dust we will return.

Our faith teaches us,
That impossible is nothing,
And mountains are stepping stones for us to see the world clearly,
And oceans just a little puddle to clean our feet,
And most importantly,
It tells us....
We are the champions of the world.

DIRGE

    sonorous and joyful chorus,
How you have deserted me,
    lofty and peaceful thoughts,
How you have fled from me,
How bare and depleted my soul is.

    grim-reaper of souls,
Why do thou haunt me so?
    cursed pitch-forked guardian of hell,
Why do thou also torment me so?
Tearing my very being and essence apart.

What more can I offer?
What price do I still have to pay?
My heart can bleed no more,
As my soul ache for a long lost respite,
Accepting and eagerly embracing death's olive branch.

JIGSAW PUZZLE

Life……..,
So happy,
But yet so unhappy,
So funny,
But yet so annoying,
So easy,
But yet so difficult.

Life……….,
What is it all about?
The joy or the sadness,
The fulfilment (of dreams),
Or the un-fulfillment,
The sweet aphrodisiac of love,
Or the scathing bitterness of hatred.

If only……..,
The secrets of life,
Could be placed in my hands,
So that to very option placed before me,
I would be wise enough to choose the better
of the options,
Then,
Life won't be a compendium,
A jigsaw puzzle,
With a tiny pertinent piece amiss.

HAPPINESS

A resonating gloom,
Glares deep inward into my heart,
A promise of an unnerving doom,
Sprouts like an angel of death,
As it come valiantly to collect my soul.

My strength fails me miserably,
My belief and faith dwindles like a heath,
My eyes scour around desperately,
For a respite out of this dearth,
From where will my escape apparate from?

Like Robin of Locksley in the dreaded forest,
My memories fire an emblazon arrow,
A pathway to my imminent rest,
And tears oozes freely from my eyes like a water-logged furrow,
And my happiness all tucked away in my memories gets unleashed.

CRUSHED

A damning fixation,
A ruse of emotion,
Like a burning train,
That barrages the brain,
And reasoning becomes inept.

I shudder at the thought of what could be,
Without striving to attain what can be,
Fear and obsession take over,
As confidence dashes for cover,
And a way forward eludes me.

Why is it so complicated?
Or are my thoughts just over-rated,
There is neither a winner nor loser,
Just the crushed and the crusher,
And a world of uncertainty and what-ifs.

Continuous thoughts bring forth no answers,
Continuous denial is no path-finder either,
Living in the moment seems the right option,
Embracing my emotional loss….. A viable action,
As I plunge into my reality of crushed infatuation.

CHOICES

In the midst of our joy,
Lies our sorrow,
In the midst of our happiness,
Lies our unhappiness,
In the midst of our bliss,
Lies our pain,
In the midst of our laughter,
Lies our weeping,
In the midst of our fertility,
Lies our mortality,
In the midst of our wisdom,
Lies our foolishness,
In the midst of our trust,
Lies our betrayal,
In the midst of our love,
Lies our hatred.

In the midst of all these,
There I lie, Confused and frustrated,
Thrown in the thick abyss of a paradoxical world,
Holding on to the glimmer of hope,
That in the midst of all these senselessness,
There is a path of reasoning,
That lies before me,
To guide and lead me forth,
Through the machinations of these confused world,
Teaching me its tenets and values.

DAYS

There were days,
Days spent with friends and loved ones,
Days hanging around foes and sycophants,
Days filled with bitterness,
Days of inebriation and cluelessness.

Of all these days,
Days spent in your company remain my most memorable days,
They came upon me so quietly,
Like a gentle spirit consuming my being,
Taking control and never wanting to leave.

To every start there's an end,
To every morning there's a night,
Coming upon us so fast we never knew,
Like a deadly thief in the night,
So has our end come upon us?

My heart grows numb,
And words can't describe these pain I feel,
Yet I bear you no grudge,
For deep inside,
I remain thankful for those days with you.

ADULATION

The early morning light raises my eye-lids,
A beautiful day was being born,
A wonderful morning is been unfolded,
And for this wonderful events,
I give Him all the glory.

My tears wiped off,
My struggles brought to an end,
My sadness vaporized,
And once again,
I praise His name.

I fail at being a yardstick for holiness,
I fall short of being prayerful,
My importance is the least of the billions walking the earth,
But still,
He abides with me in all.

His promises to me never fails,
His protection is impeccable,
His love for me never falters,
And for this,
I will forever worship at His feet.

He blots out my transgressions,
Overwhelming me with His grace,
His mercies embarrasses me,
And like the father He is,

I remain tuckered in His arms.

He is the Lord of all Lords,
He is the one called I AM,
He is the author and the finisher,
And His kingdom shall forever reign,
He is my God and my King.

POKER FACE

Nothing is what it seems to be,
The disparity of life amazes me,
I am flummoxed.....yes, startled,
And my perception of life sullied,
While I ponder answers to the confounding.

Roaring silence deafens me,
And open masks frightens me,
Most times, I'm stuck at an interception,
Trying to go beyond obstructions,
While I perpetually glean the embers of life.

I'm tired of living a lie,
The smile I wear thins out as I die,
A result of the cravings that I feel,
The gaping vacuum I want to fill,
The utopian world I desperately cringe for.

I'm sick of the prejudice,
Blitzed by the injustice,
That embellish the grueling machinations of life,
If I could discard the jejune feelings of being alive,
And embrace the jocund warmth of nature.

LOVE

So much ado about love,
A deluge of emotions,
Making one's head to hover,
Like a burning fiery lotion,
Tormenting one's soul.

My brilliance and intelligence,
Lays to waste in utter abasement,
A shocking besmirch on my haughty delusions,
Awaiting me is a rude awakening and chastisement,
A blessing I foolishly grasp.

I succumb and kneel in humble penance,
As the lesson of heart over mind seeps in,
And I revel in this mysterious instance,
As the magic of love finally sinks in,
A mystery the mind deems unfathomable.

LIFE

It could be kind and beautiful,
It could be harsh and ugly,
It could be gentle and smooth,
It could be thorny and rough,
It could be soft and easy,
It could be hard and difficult,
Whatever life is for you,
It still remains an amazing journey,
One you must live fully,
Life is whatever you make of it,
And we make the choices we create.

THE PAIN BARRIER

It feels so faint and distant,
Yet it hits me so hard,
The pain numbs my soul,
And my body creaks under such burden,
Leaving my spirit broken and sore.

Like a lone sailor,
Battling against an oncoming tide,
I flinch not at the outpour of the sea,
But at finding the current of solace,
On whose trail I shall glide.

That my heart might soar,
My soul freed from the bodily caste,
And my fears vanquished,
As the waves of pain engulfs me,
And my breath seized probably for the
penultimate time.

WONDER WOMAN

Her eyes all swollen and puffy,
The dark corners artistically filtered off,
Worn on an ethereal smile,
And striding with a chic sashay,
That buries the voiceless pain.

She feels used and trampled upon,
Her resolve worn out and abused,
Dejection becomes a theme,
As depression lurks in the periphery,
And self-esteem abdicates.

If she could know,
Of what courage lies deep within,
Of the mesmerizing beauty she possess,
Of the admiration that trails her every step,
If she could only know,
How special and magnificent she truly is.

THE FORLORN STRANGER

He walks by every day,
Looking so lovely and elegant,
His clothes well ironed and impeccable,
Taking grateful strides like he's in a ballet recital,
One could sing along with his every step,
What an epitome of the good life.

Not even a glance at the infatuated belles' ogling,
Not the slightest care for the hustle and bustle of the city,
Just a friendly nod to acknowledge the greetings of neighbors,
And from the look on his face,
One could tell a million stories,
You could swear they would all have happy endings.

A wry smile crosses his lips,
As he strolls by,
And in his eyes,
There's a tingle of excitement dancing a flummoxed waltz,
One could say he has a story to tell,
One that will fascinate his listeners.

If only we could stare deeper and see his heart,

Listen to the tears that seems to drown it,
If we could hear of his anguish and desolation,
See the worries and sadness that plagues him,
Feel the pain and loneliness that burdens him,
Then we'll understand the silent stroll he takes daily.

THE ILLUSION

A funny story life is,
A comical creature man is,
A perfect union of the two,
Births a savage man placed in an upsy-turvy world,
Where everything and nothing seems to matter.

Savage man,
Placed in a world where everything is labelled,
Either by societal values and culture,
Labelled by religious and constitutional rights,
Or by ethnic background or family status.

Savage man,
Placed in a world where everything he does is judged,
And all who judges him are equally judged,
With an equal dose of callousness and sycophancy,
And the vicious cycle of hypocrisy rolls on.

Savage man,
Placed in a world where confusion is rife,
And uncertainty is the badge of honor,
And hope is a sales man's tool,

An opium for the hopelessness that plagues the world.

    Savage man,
Placed in a world where at the end,
It matters not the tag you carry,
Or the judgment you have received,
For dust are we,
And dust we shall become.

THE ULTIMATE GIFT

Some call them the wonders of the world,
Some.... It's the amazing beauties of the world,
The hanging gardens of Babylon,
The captivating painting of Mona Lisa,
Or the legendary Eiffel Tower,
You dare not argue with the claim,
Such beauties……..such mind astounding creations,
Soul ravishing and breath-taking.

If these could cause such amazement,
How much more the unexplained mysteries,
The swaying pantomime of the oceans,
No human ever danced ever so gracefully,
The golden beam of the dusk and dawn,
No light ever illuminated the world so beautifully,
The heart-warming smile from a stranger that brightened your day,
The reverberating innocence of a baby's cackle,
So ethereal, so pukka,
The undying affection of a mother,
That melts even the coldest and hardest of hearts.

How I wish I could go on,
I would run out of ink and note pad,

But amongst everything,
One stands out as the most amazing,
The most gracious and loveliest,
And through it,
We are availed the grace to see the diverse wonders,
And beauties that abounds our world,
The chance to waltz with the waves,
The grace to be the stranger with the heart-warming smile,
The opportunity to bathe in the glory of the illuminating dawn and dusk,
The chance to be a parent with the undying ineffable love,
The grace to behold and marvel at a baby's cackle,
The privilege of rising every morning,
Basking in the euphoria of the warmth and chaos of the day,
None can be greater nor more beautiful nor more gracious,
None can rival the greatest gift of all,
The gift of LIFE.

La Vie Est Belle (Life is Beautiful)......

THE DOLOROUS HYMN

Far cries and distant echoes,
Bring forth my wailing and heartache,
And my memories surge like a charging throe,
Bringing with a burgeoning avalanche of headache,
And royally donning on me a crown of weariness.

Dazed and immersed in a whirlpool of my confusion,
Logic and philosophy belies my illation,
As I stride into an alcove of depression,
And get hit by a catatonic bout of delusion,
Which overwhelms my being.

I long for my reincarnation,
To peel away the haunting mask I painfully wear,
To flee from the nadir of my creation,
And the torment my soul gently bears,
The apocalypse of my very essence.

Life remains shrouded in a confounding mystery,
And the truth remains a far-fetched illusion,
While the reality of life seems so surreal,
Our guiding belief no different from our scorned unbelief,

Rendering life nothing more than a tragic satire.

THE PAST

The door swung by so fast,
So ferocious I could hear its cackle as it whizzed by,
My outstretched arm hastily recoiled,
And I halt my steps with an equal dexterity,
Not sure if I should advance forward.

I wonder what lies behind the door,
Making it so threatening and menacing,
Adorning its edges with veils of uncertainty,
And constructing a walk-way paved with doubts,
Availing it a fearful force to swing with.

I long to go back through the door,
And see what changes has come over the other side,
Like Lot's wife....my heart races back,
But the thought of turning into a pillar of salt,
Glues my feet to the spot I stand.

Curiosity kills the cat they say,
The past is called that for a reason,
My path should be ahead as I set eyes on my future,
And not behind as the past woos me,
Deceiving me with its illusion of beauty.

VIRTUE

Sauntering through the dark alley,
Meandering to the high valley,
Searching for a glimmer of light,
A shimmering beacon of sight,
A leeway to future hope.

Burgeoning profanity,
Culminating in a culture of palpable vanity,
Decadence of moral values,
And dearth of virtue,
An abysmal triumph of obscenity.

My heart lingers for a moral swansong,
The sharpness of virtue's prong,
A rebirth of morality,
A return to righteous civility,
An acknowledgement of virtue in our society.

"Virtue is often praised, but most often neglected"............ Publius Syrus (Roman State-man)

MY THUMBELINA

The deafening cries,
Like an eruption from Mount Vesuvius,
But one highly anticipated and welcomed,
As the sweat beads trickle down,
And my face creases with a big grin.

So tiny and chaste,
I remain astounded,
So beautiful and royal,
I'm inexpressible confounded,
At the magic that just beautified my life.

Bone of my bones,
Flesh of my flesh,
A diamond crown to my hustles,
I gently whisper,
As I hold you in my arms,
Forever cradling you with love.

SMITTEN

She's a desirable poison,
A damning pleasure,
An endearing affliction,
Her sight gives my heart seizure,
A gift to the world from the Creator.

She's a calming influence,
On my raging bitterness and resentment,
A soothing antidote,
To my debilitating ailment,
I become a caricature without her.

    silly heart,
How you have fallen,
Your pride left with no breath,
And your world so smitten,
A feat only an angel could ever do to you.

THE TRAGEDY OF MY HEART

I can't really explain what I feel,
I guess some would call it love,
And would explain it as what brightens their heart,
But for me,
I consider it the damnation of my soul,
Not the eternal damnation of the spiritual soul,
But something mortally worse,
It destroys you while you yet live,
Taking hostage of your cognitive abilities,
And filling your senses with happiness,
But when it departs from you,
It wrenches your soul apart,
And the emotional demon wrecks it havoc on the physical vessel of your body,
And we begin to wonder and ponder where it all went wrong,
We re-live and replay the relationship charade,
And dig ourselves deeper into the pit of depression,
But rather than despise that which has been the agent of our depression,
We still miss it and yearn for it,
So that when the emotional door opens up to us again,
We selfishly and stupidly board the train again,

And hold on to it tenaciously like a drug addict on his fix,
Ignoring the torture of depression we just escaped,
And we live the façade all over again,
Maybe that's why they call it love,
But for my humble self,
It is the death of my emotional soul,
The tragedy of my heart.

AFRICA

Africa,
Land of my father,
Land of my origin,
The best of all continents,
Specially created and blessed by the
Supreme One.

Africa,
Land of my mother,
Been through pains and so much,
But still stood the test of time,
To come and rule,
He shall be stronger than a thousand Roman
Empire,
And reign for as long as this world survives.

But first,
There must be remission,
There must be cleansing,
All unfit elements must be washed off,
And a new Africa shall emerge.

Africa,
Land of my struggle,
That has been through rebirth,
A new face shall it portray to the world,
Hope to all and sundry resuscitated,
And a new world order of peace begins.

Africa,
My future,
My past,
My present,
The future of Africa begins now.

MIST

They say after every dark cloud,
There's a silver lining,
After every storm,
There comes clarity,
But this only brings hope,
To those who can survive the hard times.

At this point many questions arises,
What if I don't make it?
What if the silver lining never comes?
What if the clarity remains a mist?
What if all hope is lost.

Every morning spells a worse beginning,
And makes me wish it never begun,
I become an epitome of suffering,
A paragon of ill-luck,
The work of a great Kunstler.

My life crashes before me,
Shedding an unquestionable doubt about my future,
I begin to take to the pessimistic side of life,
And believe the negative things said about me,
Rather than the positive.
I'm at a loss of what is right or wrong,
And at a point,
Wish I was never born,

Frustration seems to be a companion,
And sadness seems to decussate my path.

Like a Schleicher,
Life maneuvers me,
Dandy-ness, gaiety and the likes,
Goes extinct in my vocabulary,
And only Him who created me,
Can now rescue me.

DECADES

Decades have passed,
Since I first yearned,
For the arms of another,
Since I first sought,
For solace in the bosom of another.

Decades have passed,
But none has compared,
To your soothing touch,
Warming my body as I lay on the couch,
Caressing the essence of my being.

Decades have passed,
And decades will still pass,
But none shall have my heart,
As you have secured my heart,
For you are and will always be,
My one eternal love.

INNER DEMONS

You know not the anguish I feel,
The sorrow that lies within,
Of the vacuum I long to fill,
Or the fiery depression ever burning,
That leaves the soul scarred and bare.

You hear not my wailing chorus,
Nor the haunting shrieks of my dreams,
Drowned with the sepulcher sobs oozing from
my eyes like pus,
And the sorrowful sighs that feels like
beams,
As pain becomes my compass.

All you see is the smile I wear,
That hides a mortified face,
All you hear is the chuckle of fear,
Constantly confused with a cackle of grace,
If only my heart could open up,
So you'll see the horror that torments it.

NUMB

And the illusions,
Like a fragile glass,
Shatters into a million fragments,
And the ethereal endearment,
Gets concocted with vile reality.

Like a shot through the head,
A slap to the face,
An arrow to the heart,
The cold cloud of reality,
Envelopes my consciousness.

The surreal undertone,
The sweet and sour awakening,
The numb emotions,
Gently tugs at my soul,
Before slipping away to oblivion,
And I feel no more.

DOXOLOGY

The breaking of dawn,
The rooster crowing,
And like the waves in an ocean,
The morning comes creeping,
A new day is upon me.

A closet of good tidings,
A shower of disappointment,
A meal of success-topping,
A sip of contentment,
I step out into the sunlight reinvigorated.

Success or failure,
Smiles or tears,
Pain or pleasure,
Life is a double dose attire I wear,
An experience I'm eternally grateful for.

MY MUSE

Dreams and illusions are nothing but a mirage,
A façade to delight the inebriated,
No different from the myth of love,
An aphrodisiac to the heart of the young,
An oasis in the desert of life.

The rigor of reality taunts me,
The memories of the past haunts me,
The uncertainty of the future ridicules me,
Yet my soul leaps for joy,
And the arduous nature of life fazes me not.

Like the three saints of Dante,
Guiding him in his descent through hell,
I have you as my saint,
Guiding me through the journey of life,
Inspiring me to greatness.

Armed with a smile that thaws the ice of worries,
A touch that soothes away my stress,
A face that mesmerizes my depression,
A voice that instills the sweetest of dreams,
You have become my muse.

ODE TO A FRIEND

My eyes still hurt,
My heart has been stung,
I ponder what life is worth,
As the hope gets burnt,
And belief in good is flayed.

I reach for the past,
Longing for mem'ries held dear,
Hoping for a chance for one more blast,
A reunion without tears,
Rather of smile and laughter.

The grim reaper calls once more,
As the cold shudder of death grips me,
Life becomes a teasing bore,
Laced with a continuous sting of the bee,
I say adieu old friend.

THE ROMANTIC

"Nearest is dearest",
The Sages once argued,
"Distance makes the heart grow fonder",
The Philosophers retorted,
And for centuries,
These words have stood,
Conflicting the heart of the romantic.

For so long,
I have fought valiantly,
And defended staunchly the tenets of the sages,
Holding close to my heart,
Those their presence consoles me,
And with the littlest regard,
For those who are farthest from me.

But when you came along,
My loyalty for the sages waned,
And I sung a new mantra,
Cos my heart is being held captive,
By the soul of one,
Who is neither a Sage nor a Philosopher,
And either nearest or farthest matters,
For wherever you are,
There my heart will be.

BATTLEFIELD ODE

Whoosh...............phew,
That's the sound of a bullet,
As it fizzles past my ear,
Colliding with the nearby embankment,
Just gently resting beside me,
How the bullet escaped me,
I still remain ignorant of.

Dutifully donning my head gear,
And my well-fitted camouflage khaki,
My muzzled rifle hoisted above my shoulders,
I earnestly and fervently march on,
With my eyes alert and edgy,
Whilst choking away the whistle of death,
As it eerily buzzes around me.

How I got here,
I honestly do not care,
Only how I leave constantly tug at my head,
Why I'm here,
Seems so irrelevant and inconsequential,
Only my desired victory against the antagonist,
Spurs my every step.

Whoosh...............Bang,
That's the sound of my bullet,
Smashing the enemy's skull,

I release an exhilarating sigh and take a deep breath,
And hurriedly brush off my khaki,
As I march into the distant sight,
With the groans of men as my marching lullaby.

THE PILGRIM'S BAGGAGE

I huffed and puffed,
Strutting against the brute pavement,
My energy completely blitzed,
My face furrowed in disappointment,
As I ponder the hands of fate dealt to me.

Helplessly did I saunter,
My heart heavy with palpable dolor,
And my feeble outstretched hands teeters,
As I reach for an invisible succor,
Grappling at the wisp of air.

My eyes look out searching,
Desperate for a silver lining,
A reason to keep on breathing,
A cause to keep hoping,
A chance to be and feel alive.

THE DEMISE

A seething hopelessness,
Leaves me plunging,
Into a quagmire of dolefulness,
Accompanied by nothing else save my screaming,
And a grief-stricken heart.

Restitution I craved not,
Neither do my misery desire companion(s),
As I wallowed in my rot,
Taking solace in my delusion,
Haughtily awaiting the grim reaper.

How has this fate befallen me?
My head continues to ponder,
As the end truly beckons to me,
And my frail body whimpers,
As the cold jaw of death envelopes me.